Orphic
Politics

BOOKS BY TIM LILBURN

POETRY

Names of God (1986)

From the Great Above She Opened Her Ear to the Great Below
    (with Susan Shantz) (1988)

Tourist to Ecstasy (1989)

Moosewood Sandhills (1994)

To the River (1999)

Kill-site (2003)

Desire Never Leaves: The Poetry of Tim Lilburn (with Alison Calder) (2007)

Orphic Politics (2008)

ESSAYS

Poetry and Knowing: Speculative Essays and Interviews (editor) (1995)

Living in the World as If It Were Home (1999)

Thinking and Singing: Poetry and the Practice of Philosophy (editor) (2002)

Orphic —— Politics

poems

Tim Lilburn

McCLELLAND & STEWART

LIBRARY AND ARCHIVES CANADA CATALOGUING IN PUBLICATION

Lilburn, Tim, 1950–
 Orphic politics : poems / Tim Lilburn.

ISBN 978-0-7710-4636-0

I. Title.

PS8573.I427O76 2008   C811'.54   C2007-905935-X

We acknowledge the financial support of the Government of Canada
through the Book Publishing Industry Development Program and that of the
Government of Ontario through the Ontario Media Development
Corporation's Ontario Book Initiative. We further acknowledge the support
of the Canada Council for the Arts and the Ontario Arts Council for our
publishing program.

Typeset in Golden Cockerel by M&S, Toronto
Printed and bound in Canada

This book is printed on acid-free paper that is
100% recycled, ancient-forest friendly.

McClelland & Stewart Ltd.
75 Sherbourne Street
Toronto, Ontario
M5A 2P9
www.mcclelland.com

1   2   3   4   5   12   11   10   09   08

CONTENTS

Orphic
Politics

GETTING SICK

I dug a slot into the gravel of no address,
I dug a slot warm as a hand into the air's water-cliff.
The eye seeing me is a charred-wood-backed river cannonballing
through badlands   badly disciplined, lizardly hills, water in mitres
of cinder freighting necessity's weight past my head on the ground
                                                    sleeping,
the eye's windy mouth, love-yanked night wall; pines triple axel in it.
Coal-masked generosity, no name.

        *   *   *

Two years we were stubbed on the floor, bone-eared, smoke-cheeked.
Urgency, in a torn gown, held my chin between its thumb and
    index finger and unreined its face lunging
into my face, its face a foot from mine cataracted, and said
a single word a day from a pack of ten.
I put my finger in its mouth and, then, sick, was triaged
up barely blacksmithed, leprechaun, lignin creeks
that were unloading the hills,
its nose a foot from my face,
bonemeal, burnt wire creeks,
flicker of antler, thinlipped cat, graphite dust, no cartilage
creeks, I followed them up, with a bag of roasted sand, bag
of swung sticks, pushed in a shopping cart, building materials for the
    very top, the static of Europe bulging my knee.
I dug a slot into no address,

my knee geigered a snailheaded ghost, an unread Chaldean library
below the hover of Plato's soul.
In small stone houses, violet fields were artillerying from a century ago
under the floors.

ORPHIC HYMN

It salmons from leagues of leafmulch
                    and writhes to the door.
Oak leaf shadow craters its spine range and neck
    as if it walked between being's lit breasts and the screen.
It's got caught, opened in its antlers, the wood-covered 16th century book
that works out I am sick.
I hold this up to what I am doing, lying on the divan, haven't pissed
or shit in days, infection's horse's rider lashes back and forth
with his black flag. Two winter stars with dessert plate heads
two months ago were nailed at either edge of my groin.
I've been pensioned a shield of bees
below my chin, under earliest skin, a bridge, a sleeve of industry.
The MRI tech asked if I like country or classical.
The dogwood tree blooms in the full window a rising whine.
The temperature of this nuzzles in like sediment that's already stone.
A knife waits, girlish, down the hill, flipping over, over, small
    fish flash at the bottom of that boat, convinced, the knife, crossing
and uncrossing its legs.

A SURGERY AGAINST ANGELISM

Set a fat layer of fire grazing into the chest of engine heat, breast-
stroking against motion perfuming from the sickness of volt swollen
                              inhalations. Let this heat
sag to a half-eaten meal not its own; let it eat rods,
iron shavings, green stones, dead yarrow, words headfirsting
from a rock overhang in the upper right, a skeleton of a seal; let it learn
        to heave-hiss through its mouth the complete psalmic blade.
Five pound fire gravities against hurtling's musk.
In the chest of engine heat, a concussed floor;
whipped light-heads cough in blows' trampoline, and choir above
    their husks, they lurch into a blurred but, yes, readable circle, moving,
        yes, the gear that jacks the cranial dome.
You go into the fish's mouth which is Siberian citizenship,
into the fish's mouth which is the body of a cousin
                              at the volcano's wedding.
We come out of the upper colon tunnel onto the ledge, sweet-looking
    antlers to smoke from the cloud deer. We've built a shack
                              out of this numbnutsness,
    we've hidden in this long grass. A stick will cure us.
Your eyes in the fish's gut are moved like a wand around the dark.
The knife snugs down through skin.   And this is politics.

4

Momentum's needle pulls the ear in its elm bark casket
                                under four and a half feet of ice,
past alder-leaf-hide windows, where it sweats shaking, bony rooms
of West European night which hydraulic over seventy-two hours
a rack from themselves that is the corpus of the lake
in armspread thinking, then the rooms, their singlebed ears, breast up
points of sparking sentence-skeletons of tamarack, of cougar-wound rock,
      one bird opening in a canyon
                                        stuffing miles into mass.
This is Tristia, here *serviam*'s darling pubic mound. Set the table.
Roman-candling around the henosised ear, towering nose,
pheromones of the aquatic cat; a squirrel plays dead in the green
                                 cloud, bottom-dipping smell.
A birch's drifting claw is caught in ice.
The tusked fish cuts and cuts over the sludge.
The ear dragged by moaning chains, gang-followed, in its quiet.

THICKNESS, TRAVELLING

Flying forward, hard, down, horse-blur,
afternoon-mouthed locust clatter, then the doors, buttering
                                    with weight,
went to the doors again, falling was pounded into all the fissures,
gravity's crammed stalks, gravity's slanting gravel barley field.
Parkade-scraped, diesel-soaked, the weight-flowering doors.
A hand seals itself to the collagened locks, the walls javelined three
quarters of an inch when whitewater-gowned torsos snicked through
Randy's skull, panels of wet burnt logs, panels of waist length hair.
Amphorae, coke cans, the mountain sliding away,
decaying with sadness, gravity-bloom belonging to no one.
And the eyes in the doors, algae-shag, hoppings of algae,
gas in the doors' eddies.
And the doors lifted their eyes
            like hands to me.
And the brown trout dirty jerk of morphine moved under,
wolverine smile of deepening skin,
nosing in mineral clarity to what it knew: the walled city
            where maybe ten oil lamps laboured in all the towers.

IF METAPHOR IS THEURGY, IT MUST FORM

The Divine Comedy, its crane beak sheening, the rusted
paring knife skull cap, bambooed sexual legs payloading and floating
                              in flax stubble, like someone
unpacking a picnic, unfolds a cloth of itself, a map, fifteen feet under
him in kneading air over black rock, pumping landing lights of the map
passing through steam clouds from vents, and turning on it musically,
                              on the turntable of the book,
is the valley and seventeen inch neck farm of the *Summa Theologica*,
Parmenides' white horse,
and the *Summa* again, eighty pounds of eyes in a square lit like
a wrestling ring, the eggwhites castle of Aristoteleanism, which, un-
crossing its arms, monstrances itself as a reed boat smoothing through
crow-smoke and palms barging the loudly oiled, drive-in-movie-screen
                              forehead of Christianity
on a red leather Hausa cushion.
And Proclus, hidden in alders, in his cat voice, hems this into the skin,
where its eye-gold is chewed and the night man's
body turns into a field of the poem's shivering, afterlife wheat
and this is politics too, and the true right-armed city grows
in his skin-boat convulsing,
and he smells the wool-sock-drying-on-a-radiator smell
of the mountain around him.

Pythagoras, sliced, freezered cat, defrocked Wal-Mart greeter, in
   anachoresis, face welted with interior mountainings, mountain
               whippings, grinds ahead, dolphining,
                        dolphining,
in and out of the artifact-cavitied humus of the Chukatcha Peninsula,
a curly iron basket of oily fire at the bulb of his forehead; he
               is stitching, you can imagine a gold thread
leaking and spinning braided from his testicles.
See him in the horsetail headdress of Apollo, a loaned snake cape, his
               look has the gargly Cessna
roar of one moony engine leaving the continental shelf at night in snow,
this is the real one-father, bobbing in greasy light, then he
drops behind a metre high gravel ridge and night is there;
the Bering Sea rotates its nineteenth century gear inside
the drum of herony, idle volcanoes, toenail painting, Las Vegased,
                    dishy volcanoes,
near which all the Pythagoreans sweat.
So you want to go home but haven't a clue.
Here's one, a ganglion.
Recall that the ciliced, winded thigh will go by its own delectation
                   into the flint trench
That the whale bones must cover the corpse completely
That the water creeping down in stones on this body is the sky bull
OK, now to go into the rolling mouth, take the stubbly, mud stairs
up to the surgery ward and through it, wiping gecko webs
                   from the i.v. trees,
then into the broom closet that rustles with mammoth bones.

Now slide your soon-to-be-sliced thigh into the slate-sliding water,
go down in it, there is a promised house inside exactly the size of your
head, abdomen, legs, a book within a book, book written
                                    on the inside and on the outside,
a key shape outlined by a stitch of white stones on the intertidal plain.

"You'll have to understand, beautiful boy, that the previous speech was by Phaedrus, Pythocles' son, from Myrrhinous, while the one I am about to deliver is by Steisichorus, Euphemus' son, from Himeria [Steisichorus, son of Good Speaker, from the Land of Desire].

"'There is no truth to that story' – that when a lover is available you should give your favors to a man who doesn't love you instead, because he is in control of himself while the lover has lost his head. That would have been fine to say if madness were bad, pure and simple; but in fact the best things we have come from madness, when it is given as a gift of the god.

"The prophetess of Delphi and the priestesses at Dodona are out of their minds when they perform that fine work of theirs for all of Greece, either for an individual person or for a whole city, but they accomplish little or nothing when they are in control of themselves. We will not mention the Sybil or the others who foretell many things by means of god-inspired prophetic trances and give sound guidance to many people – that would take too much time for a point that's obvious to everyone. But here's some evidence worth adding to our case: The people who designed our language in the old days never thought of madness as something to be ashamed of or worthy of blame; otherwise they would not have used the word 'manic' for the finest experts of all – the ones who tell the future – thereby weaving insanity into prophecy. They thought it was wonderful when it came as a gift from the god, and that's why they gave its name to prophecy; but nowadays people don't know the fine points, so they stick in a 't' and call it 'mantic'. ...

"Next, madness can provide relief from the greatest plagues of trouble that beset certain families because of their guilt for ancient crimes: it turns up among those who need a way out; it gives prophecies and takes refuge in prayers to the gods and in worship, discovering mystic rites and purifications that bring the man it touches through to safety for this and all time to come. So it is that the right sort of madness finds relief from present hardships for a man it has possessed."

Phaedrus, 244a–245a

MEETING THE ANGEL, TASTING WHAT IT SEES

I
Ten yards of mineral hair fall inside the cruciform hummingbird,
inside these unthrottled, ox-bearded shoulders of wasps.
Egyptian quail, the Orient of the quail, are a ringed hand
                              swum over this strangled grass,
the stone jaws of dragonflies, sleep's hinge over this near-fire
                                                  ground.
The falling inside everything is cymballing nudity,
                              cosmos-reciting ladder.
Now is in the cougar's mouth.
Look at these ferns. See, your hand goes into their side.
The gods bleed into dead leaves, bark, pieces of tile,
                              stab their bodies in, behind their slate windows.
The wasps with lavender scales touch it, in jade earflares
                              nose-bunt the near-fire ground.
The falling inside everything is tranced, encyclopedic nudity,
                                        cymballing ladder.
The infected antennae of wasps, arced, terracotta
        wasps, their asphalt pyramid eyes.
A feathered, concussing suck and you are in the operating theatre light
        muscle of plucked ignorance, gowned in your lowest face, this
is meeting the angel, angelicity
is your lotteried face, chloroformed but bright, fruited into you.
The angel cuts in, scooping over, its odour an early metal,
possibilities, burnt strips of paper, coldhammered inside.

II

Then I went along the Amur River,
chert in my elbow, a grasshopper ligature bucking the end
of my tongue.
Blackened yellow spiders, boomboxing forms, big as zucchini,
                              small dogs,
                    Theoren Fleury on a kicked-in night, squinting along;
behind my calves, ants hatted with three wings.
I went ahead on a Levallois knee.
I portaged the summa painting of religion, 4x6 glass,
through it September 2, 2005, afternoon, rain prinking down in Loss
Creek, alder leaves in stopped, oil-coloured water, stones with winter
like a boat tied up in them.
Amur River, moulting eye, saying itself into
the mouth of reindeer moss, moths and bats lariating in ash.
I was walking, hiding the mind's kissable sword.
I was thinking of al-Ghazali, so what, blood pressing the nail,
                              I was walking.
I let Pico della Mirandola slow his limbs humming
      through my hair, why not, I knew where the elands bunched,
how they went through the rain crevice.
I knew their smoke and what to say.
Right along the Amur River, hovelling in the sword.
And then from the beach I slid into the glacier-eyed
fish.

III

Ten yards of moonless hair herniate inside the cruciform
                              hummingbird, then well from its green belly.
And inside you, Enkidu, ibex-nosed, streamchested, the Friend,
                   midden-pong, satanically muscled, tips,
          stilting on a column of erasures and forgettings.
Inside you, Enkidu, his hospital pudding legs, the shoulders
     with forest dark and seal stares copulated right out of them.
One deer, its side sawed away, Kawasaki-leaning close to rock over dry
leaves through bramble, slants toward this caving to salt the damp of
tremor out of it, so that it can glide-collapse, engine off,
in radio silence, into the siphoning ear of this angel, this
one, a drinking under the skin, this one, which has come, its
tongue blood-glued hummingbird feathers,
its hand, dried, sutured, rattling flint sparks of individuation.

My mother puts fleabane near her mouth
and small farms suck down in feathery roars,
tipping like ocean liners, grass roofs, poplar poll barns
lifted then slanting down in pillaring dust.
Sand curtains buckle into the room.
She puts roads on her arms, brome overhanging them,
grasshoppers flawlessly clearing the roads.
Pull the car over on this approach; don't worry about the grass
clawing the oil pan; now go into the trees, a clattering bouquet of pails,
blindfolded berries, you've heard, near the slough, mosquitoes
                                        big as sparrows.
My mother's upper lip is mosquitoed shade.
Steam engines plough into the earth
slamming one foot, seven feet under, between Creelman, Sask. and
                                        Fillmore, Sask.,
cream cans rolling, routering down,
cars falling the height of buildings; there they meet the crown-
            dragging, always-turning, lacustrine-clay-edemaed buffalo.
Wheat from 1942 trickles down
    the rat hole of the engines and bibles, too,
fall down the hole and hymnals.
My mother puts the moth of light inside the lamp.
My mother asks the day what day it is, and her brother jerks out of
                the Kipling Legion on a Dieppe raid leg,
cannoning the tune of lymphatic cancer to everyone on the prairies,
his harrowed, wobble-faced guitar, strands weaseled from the screen
                door, August 1933.
My mother the gold dragonfly, gold entering
        green near the spine.

He sleep-otters under small black stones that are in
    porcupine skins of fire in long Hegelian hair.
He is gouged and loosened by the swaying in his mouth,
he is fattened by the fats of the larger fish-tailing mouth, and
illness' knapped letter is ribboned to his elbow.
In the water-earth, the gonging, sliding brown of the pine forest
upside down; he will bring us back a shimmering report,
the big meal where we are brought out as buried sons.
His penis is periscoped, the wrists grind the shale boat's oar.
And now he is before the blueness of the lower curve of the bicep
inside the lowing stones, inside the cloud-dipping rock.
He runs the tongue of his seeing along the architecture of a groan
inside basalt, which is a house wolverined into the ground with a
                              shoulder-high grass roof,
walls rubbed white clay where people have sex
and pray. It fevers into the Abbey of Cluny then back, voice-roofed.
It steps out of static then back into the thicket.
A house of thirty days of rain in chorally hoarse rock,
pocket-sized Louvre palming one piece of loot, ghost
of the sea's ear, leaf of paradise.
He sits down at its workbench,
the only furniture in the pounding room,
and slots his eye upon its lathe.

THEURGY

So: we came after bibles of dust fell, Alexandrias, falling concordances
of turning away, horses dragging blue gortex packs, loupes, specula
hung on hooks of clatter over streams a little back where we'd left
a cook fire, to a spreading
in the forest's fist, *Symposium* 215b–216c,
Alcibiades hammered in lurching fern, small lights, fertilized,
flying-within, clawed eggs, trellising
over water, tongue-chariots we thought,
Alcibiades ploughed, the fucker, in forepawed grass, teeth, elk
                                                    and bear,
slapping on him, a singing on his skin like an oil, a running flame
that didn't go in, the man, snot surfing from his smashed face, talking,
talking, turning to the wall, talking, turning back, talking, a buried
erection in a paleolithic hand, talking, near the dolphin (talking),
    chinless, grin-flanked, under-ocean saint-speaker,
                                the stream-naked Socrates.
This is going back.
A violin in the mouth lynx-moving under the dark.
A weather drum, sex drum under the teeth.
A man flayed, the god with a flute in the opening.
So we go back, this is going back,
this is the bread of prayer, Alcibiades elected into the drool whipping
from his mouth, he's pissed himself.
So we go back, this is going back
with the names that have no hands or feet.
Nikolai Berdyaev. Lori Niedecker.
The rilled mouthed fish-man sleep-eating in an algae cloud:

he carried a swelling Eucharist bell in his rotted throat, he
brought elbow-edged marks from snapped grass stalks in his dust

                                                          throat.

We shook.

"Now Zeus, the great commander in heaven, drives his winged chariot first in the procession, looking after everything and putting all things in order. Following him is an army of gods and spirits arranged in eleven sections. Hestia is the only one who remains at the home of the gods; all the rest of the twelve are lined up in formation, each god in command of the unit to which he is assigned. Inside heaven are many wonderful places from which to look and many aisles which the blessed gods take up and back, each seeing to his own work, while anyone who is able and wishes to do so follows along, since jealousy has no place in the god's chorus. When they go to feast at the banquet they have a steep climb to the high tier at the rim of heaven; on this slope the god's chariots move easily, since they are balanced and well under control, but the other chariots barely make it. The heaviness of the bad horse drags its charioteer toward the earth and weighs him down if he has failed to train it well, and this causes the most extreme toil and struggle that a soul will face. But when the souls we call immortals reach the top, they move outward and take their stand on the high ridge of heaven, where its circular motion carries them around as they stand while they gaze upon what is outside heaven. . . .

"Now a god's mind is nourished by intelligence and pure knowledge, as is the mind of any soul that is concerned to take in what is appropriate to it, and so it is delighted at last to be seeing what is real and watching what is true, feeding on all this and feeling wonderful, until the circular motion brings it around to where it started. On the way around it has a view of Justice as it is; it has a view of Self-control; it has a view of Knowledge – not the knowledge that is close to change, that becomes different as it knows the different things which we consider real down here. No, it is the knowledge of what really is what it is. And when the soul has seen all the things that are as they are and feasted on them, it sinks back inside heaven and goes home. On its arrival, the charioteer stables the horses by the manger, throws in ambrosia, and gives them nectar to drink besides.

"Now that is the life of the gods. As for the other souls, one that follows a god most closely, making itself most like that god, raises the head of the charioteer up to the place outside and is carried around in the circular motion with the others. Although distracted by the horses, this soul does have a view of Reality, just barely. Another soul rises at one time and falls at another, and because its horses pull it violently in different directions, it sees some real things and misses others. The remaining souls are all eagerly straining to keep up, but are unable to rise; they are carried around below the surface, trampling and striking one another as each tries to get ahead of the others. The result is terribly noisy, very sweaty, and disorderly. Many souls are crippled by the incompetence of the drivers, and many wings break much of their plumage. After so much trouble, they all leave the site of reality unsatisfied, and when they have gone they will depend on what they think is nourishment – their own opinions."

Phaedrus, 247a–248c

Cut into the tongue where the fish dive;
there's a castle there under a shallow black lake, ducks with bicycle-
                                pumped white heads,
moon-bored corridors, still lit from the first potashy coring.
Come in at 45 degrees, falling cleanly though sky, and buck down
and back, you will caravan through one glassy strata then another,
some musical, and when you lose your way in crosswinds,
                                muscle alone will be your star.
The moon-ticked, savoured body
tasted and heard as this castle.
A brother to you is the shallow, decayed water smell of
the carob syringe. The barrel goateed with strips from Deutero-Isaiah.
We will take out elm alleys and alphic hills of wheat.
Everything must be laid on gravel
and have swept over it the body-growing wing
        of unoccupied darkness,
the daemon-secreted drug.

SEE YOU

Poor fuck, I see you, your long cow teeth,
the ice cladding of your arms has poured everywhere, ice
scale of your face flowing to cast you a house or yurt.
Through its fifty below lemon gin blear I see you
alone inside in airplane position over some food's calculus,
your parsnip, *siber*, ermine face.
I notice you've hooked up with a boat of cedar-knotted femur,
carbon dated to heidelbergensis,
worthy to hold still in the sawing mare tails of the sun.
You can't speak now, your right side buried
already, you're dressed as always in whipping black.
I've become that machine, and so can see two jellyfish
the colour of the boudoir do slow martial arts for your brain.
The boat has arrived on the tip of your tongue.
The keel is spiked immediately in seven feet of prairie
just east of Rosetown but you are, yes, going.
(great starry pulling on violin-tarred ropes)

THIS, THEN

Someone wearing a vest of radon implants
coaxed my tongue to be sweetly laid out in a kurgan of rain.
This is the rain's nest, he said, where you will be joined
by the skin of a galloping horse held up by sticks.
Just then God's mouth filled with lead.
People at that time started, it seemed, to bleed
in the streets from their ears.
This wasn't force of listening, they
just were scraped by some large thing moving past,
sleet of arrows, yielding shelf of stones.
I stared at them, peak, peak, peak. The quills in their hands
and feet slicked into me, over
the border into me like I was being shot up, quietly and in secret
by drum solos.
Let us dip the tip of horror in horror.
Randy went down, Albert rappelled under the waves.
Something, all we'd never said, was eating
up from below.
St. Teresa of Avila was sitting in a gold chair
in a breathing-through-a-straw house in a suburb
quite far out, where what she's saying – it eggs slowly from
her mouth – is taken up in spikes along the back legs of the hum
                              from swelling, overhead wires.

Iamblichus to Porphyry

So then, you ask, "Why is it that many theurgical procedures are directed towards them [the daemons] as if they were subject to the passions?"

Well, my reply to that is that the question is asked out of an inexperience of sacred mystagogy. Of the works of theurgy performed on any given occasion, some have a cause that is secret and superior to all rational explanation, others are like symbols consecrated from all eternity to the higher beings, others preserve some other image ... others yet are performed in honour of their subjects, or have as their aim some sort of assimilation or establishment of familiarity. One would not, however, for all that, agree that some part of our ritual is directed toward the gods or daemons, which are the subjects of our cult as subject to passions; for that essence which is in itself eternal and incorporeal cannot itself admit any alteration emanating from bodies.

On the Mysteries (*De mysteriis*), I.11

So, in Asclepius' sanctuaries, diseases are arrested by divine dreams, and, because of the structure of nocturnal apparitions, the medical art has arisen from sacred dreams. Alexander's entire army was saved, though facing total destruction in the night, when Dionysos appeared in a dream, and this god indicated the mode of deliverance from incurable sufferings. Aphutis was also saved during King Lysander's siege, through dreams sent by Ammon, for Lysander withdrew his troops as quickly as possible, and immediately ended the siege. But why go through such occurrences one by one, when daily events offer a clarity greater than any story?

De mysteriis, III. 3

But if this divine power extends in its predictions to inanimate objects, such as little pebbles, rods, or certain woods, stones, wheat, and barley meal, this is itself the most astonishing prognostication by divine divination, because it gives life to inanimate things and motion to things motionless, and makes all clear, knowledgeable, and participating in reason ... and yet having no reason in themselves.

De mysteriis, III. 17

The water, the joke building, skeletoning up
like a clotheshorse in the ghost dust cold, 18-foot-ceilinged hall of its
reptile and cat body, the mansion water turns, it turns,
                                        its many-roomed body
turns, shoulder to fingertip side feathers rattling and licking out limely,
a door opening, a head shot, given, appearing,
or chest shot, an ovation building in the grateful prey,
                        building in the chest of water.

. . . and the Moor declared she was a Virgin
when the Logos was conceived but not, he said, carefully not,
                        roving in robes like a Jupiter moon,
after the birth, and he, the other one, battle-visioned a knife
homed twohanded into the man's chest, through the mail slot in. And
the Pilgrim, Blade, That's Theology, said
into a kissing motion in the three-plied air a foot away and up,
gluey slur, said if his mule went skating on its own will's bearings up
to the town where the man went he would kill the man, whup, whup,
but this mule did not go there,
applause cantering up in the chest of water, tongue and grooved
room of string and horn players, resting, instruments sagging,
as the San Juan River mouth body turns.

This chest shot, this opening the door, the gag of the man
with a 2x4 plank turning and turning and taking
out the guys behind, the true water billows, self-hosting, and turns
its body to us, to *us*, and the city falls, burning, and the price of diamonds

electric drills through matter like a foam-shirted Lucifer slicking
chernobylic through fat rolls of flame;
the glaciated scaling of his body scrolls up like burning roofing tile
and lifts.

We saw you! minking in armour-like felt you'd spraypainted silver,
   in the chalk street   grovelling before tomatoes, figs, visiting them
like an alien, girlfriends from a previous life, and
                            you'd lifted a piece of sod
in your garment, and allowed into you chest's inhaling-only theatre
a bird in fuchsia with a medical-looking beak, raising
the bell in your chest to enter the purple.
You'd kicked the shit beautifully out of Porphyry, everyone
   had heard this, slicing him in from the forty yard line,
                fixed, suicidal Porphyry, coming up,
as the Christian Canadians say, with your crosscheck under the visor,
and now he's looking for a slick dentist, and you're off with a handful
of his students to the hotsprings at Gadara.
Let him talk to those geniuses of racism,
Rider Haggard, Nicholas Monserrat, his eye's tongues on the beading
       of their gin hands.
Let him talk to that light-on-the-mountain Martin Heidegger.
What a winning lisp he's found.
Small stones and berries of wheat snap circularly, heat ticking down,
close to you, then behind comes the erratic of rain, the, oh, mountainous
smoke of rain, then the soul's rolling smoke.
You are so shy about your ankles, monsignor, and the dahlia cloud
you whicker into and churn in, as you quickly chant rope-pulling vowels
in that room with its bed and dark red cover, above the street that is
                                    so white.

On tongues of jammed horsetail, stacked as plates on the jaws
of fish, a scaffold of femurs and calottes staggering
from foundation posts of longhaired firepits, these,
eyes on the backs of those sturgeon, the womanly, hydrocephalic
fish stunned in a current of coaled bees.
Five o'clock shadow along this night ladder, ice's last thinking.
And, a step below, quartz bleep of knapped spark hominids
peaking along the rush of the bone ray, night
stair, moon-pulling round it, u-ed backs, the whitenesses unbending
and touching the shoulders in front, then arms shot-curved back.
Sink yourself, sew your eyes into the hole for the shark mouth
                         in a delirium cloud.
Now the nose, cavalry it into the trench up to the cliff face of the
perfume of the black feather, phallic, passed
from the slow mind of the bone to who holds it: the
                         brain tumour: given.
Tongue old as horsetail, the scent organ in your own jaw.
Beautiful city state land-lifting in the jumped nose in your jaw. That
bone hut place, pelvic roofs, a half circle in front of the bulging ice.
The bones with their welted, tripod hearts,
                    ice-scrapped breathing.
Burnt berry pits; eaten cotton hammocks.
Beneath a slate shelf in low water,
          the headlights of bones.
Stalks that move as if there were wind.

SWAN PLAIN

She drops her hands on the copper wrists of blue-green August
                                                    back gardens,
and walks, her feet in twin black ships,
in her delphiniums with her virtues. Their names writhe out of stones
in the long body of writing, except "joy" which is painted in black
inside a plywood apple nailed to a shed.
Lake stones in an old sink, a smiling particle board dog leaned behind
    hollyhocks against a two room house she's bought to tear-vial
        Co-op calendars from the 1950s.
Vegetable, turned-earth cloud lifting north, rain last night
nailing here, earth jacked by black water, getting up out of its St. Vitus
        chair, thick with rods of antenna tremble.
The Christs in the Ukrainian churches in Wroxton and Veregin
are drained to a rumbling, underground violet,
evacuated trains, moving late, thrown, below the ground,
the Christ-skin worked to the colour of pickled eggs.
Mrs. Frances Sobkow walks on fish-belly feet near the black mouth
                                                    of the north, rush
of spruce and the tart taste of hand-showing snow
in the long-organ-playing afternoon.
Some patrolling with frozen-to-the-bottom unknowing
of the back door, fragrant wormhole.
Apollo brushes his black feather along her instep near the bear meadows.
She goes down.

LYNKEUS

Plotinus, *Enneads*, V.8.4.26

I smoke-swayed into Last Mountain, the clanking dancehall cisterns,
the nunnish corridors, old lipstick coloured,
the blue mouth flame inside it, trout mouthed, idling, a berried,
                                             running-at-you
unlitness, two pelicans tipping over the scaffolding of each ear,
the mountain's blowing hole helmeting me with a blue-white caul, I
lurch-fell forward and below in a kind of crawl, cleaved dirt curl-
thrown, moaning, from the swim of shoulders, ten days to cross
the flats below Nokomis, then, when I've nosed in the twenty watt,
leafmould bed, whipped something forward with my arm,
peeking it above sleep, whipping it like a sick discus, an emotional
standing or quickness with the bony tattooedness of a dragonfly,
to smoothe under Gooseberry Lake three hundred miles southeast,
late in the twilit migrations, where it pools on its knees six
to eight months, below the rabbit stare lamps of samphire root,
in obedience to my dead who have all cleared off,
the silvery, wavery, small-mouthed family
beginning to slip-grind below ice.
I camp between the bricks and the wood
    of the house of this pleroma, the fizz-treed emanation ground.
Everyone's garden's been pickled, chickens
killed, autumn, autumn again,
the hen-dimpled yard bites down with frost.
Osculator me osculo oris sui –
Our small bed is made with flowers.
Hey, sweet Raphael Alberti, loan me your gloves.

35

Toenail, afterlife brown-white of hollyhocks in seed,
old toenail.
Bees thickening, shivering at 200 kph, losing edge, rippling with
hysteria, sipped by the straw of invisibility –
and those gloves of yours, fur-backed with bee-jitter, wet aspen
smoking, face-aromaed, antler velvet gloves. Those gloves
inner lined with an open human mouth and open birds' mouths, and
then outer coloured with plush sleep of long feathers bouncing and
dandling behind one man's beautiful forehead, these two, the feeling
of the gloves, startling, smelling of fish stooping under new ice,
the rain-shaggy, multiply tonned migrations. Inside the gloves, cities;
inside the cities, small glasses of milk. There, inside, the hearth
of the glove, in that spoken room inside the glove,
silvered up by a microbial dentist drill
on a flake of dead skin, the *Vita coetanea* of R. Llull, in barn swallow
Arabic – the part where Jesus is sledged now, now, now,
to the acrobatic, rising, peopled howl of his blood.
How long you have been from home.
Loan me those gloves, sweet eyes.

Porphyry speaks now: the creature stops and a seedhead of suppleness
                                                    forks down.
But last night, at 3:16, gas flaring
        from the red moon expressed in boils of groans and alarms,
        air-chewings from floating mouths.
All things are sewn thick with gods, whispered Iamblichus; he knew
                                        their mauve eyes; a moth
sexually palped the room, working the muscle
                of the moon being taken in,
nettles sheafed and leaning, nettles at the throat.
Next day the wedding began in the delphinium's eye.
That Adam with the mystical Eve, a folded over, folded over,
untruckable earth, erraticed in the delphinium seed, another seed,
                more wedding and weight,
                                                then a third seed,
and the gathered sticks and leaves of this, the to-be-married, holding
hands with motion that has been planed so hard the faces of herd-
        broke individuality evening-starred up in it.
The worlds mount each other and wear the clover-odoured crown.
The sun roams its mouth to the mountain.
But I also saw, mother, the fourth-rate colonial Victorian cherub
above the delphinium throb from headstone, bowing its black string.

He built the corral after he returned by a self-caused wind of fire
   in his poplar-bark sail from Constantinople, a copy of Proclus'
   Elements of Theology hand-sewn
          in his spruce-tree-line-coloured clothes.
He sang or unstabbed, or unlighteninged, the dragon-scented fence
          from small stones or earth too dry for godwits.
The sandy, forgetting corral talk-thought its way toward him, smelling
   of burnt coffee, the old nakedness of other people, heavy birds
      in October, rotting boards, three buried rings.
The fence, before it came, bull-stared at him and read him, and he
spoke it, then he read what he said, then he became this.
I don't know who he was, maybe he could jump and turn backwards
   six feet in the air, his eyeballs rolled back and he heard
    the wire tremoring hard for him and had it bloom from him,
1,068 red willow sticks tie-wired heaven to earth in it, one
   corner post a pink theurgic erratic on salt-muscled flats he'd crawled
below, punching wire below in the valley under Mankota, god-worker,
frightener of women. He pushed away old chokecherry leaves, lynx smell
and it was inside his tongue, he took away snowberry sticks
and he unbent the fence
and rolled it out in light, on-off-on, heavily coming from
the iron in little shouts.
Later I saw the fence and I could see – there is a
house inside the meat of aspens; I am sleepy thinking about it, magnetted
as if from eyes, and a room like an insect's stomach in the house;
I am sleepy thinking about the room, throat-blinded; my ear tells me it
would walk ten days to sleep there, that it wants only
to sleep there, in that room that is perfumedly there.

I lie down in the ground and bullets pass over me,
I lie down in the ground and bullets pass over me,
I lie down in the ground and dark hip flickers, dark,
    fatty air twists, physical o-o-o-o-o's, stunt over me.
Days inside the will, rooms of held rain, the recti hard
                             for Europe.
I lie down in the ground, I lie down into amnesia
        in a blur of night-streaked grass, down the moaning road.
And then I go down into the Frenchman valley from the back,
north wind bore-holing when I rise above the grass; it joys
up flint-flashes of granular cold like the twelfth century church
    sending up eros-scented ideas, and I go down to the staring
   valley badly, practised limp, coyote bones waving
      in the stammered wind.
I go there, I go there, I go there.
I lie down in the ground and bullets pass over me, I lie down
   in the ground slowly, the back of my head going first.
And the nineteenth century itself, the grand hotel of capitalism itself,
    one-nostriled, its brain a castle fireplace,
        in its gong-meringued, rose-budded, insect-licked Venetian coat,
is there, yawning, leaning back in its chair, its arms painted out
                            with night.
And Don is with me, his face red at the cheeks, and he's wearing
   a red scarf on his neck, and I stay below, looking down to where
four burning horses move along the edge of a sea.
Everything gathers and conjugalizes its animal-pelted weight
   on the point of this, so I look.

Henry Corbin

Avicenna's cycle of visionary recitals . . . situate the man Avicenna in the cosmos that the philosopher elaborated, now in such an imposing monument as the *Kitāb al-Shifā*, now in many another major and minor treatise. By substituting a dramaturgy for cosmology, the recitals guarantee the genuineness of this universe; it is veritably the place of a personally lived adventure.

Avicenna and the Visionary Recital

Muhyīddīn ibn 'Arabī

Know that when God had created Adam who was the first human organism to be constituted, and when he had established him as the origin and archetype of all human bodies, there remained a surplus of the leaven of the clay. From this surplus, God created the palm tree, so that this plant . . . is Adam's *sister*; for us, therefore, it is like an aunt on our father's side. In theology it is so described and is compared to the faithful believer. No other plant bears within it such extraordinary secrets as are hidden in this one. Now after the creation of the palm tree, there remained hidden a portion of clay from which the plant had been made; what was left was the equivalent of a sesame seed. And it was in this remainder that God laid out an immense Earth. Since he arranged in it the Throne and what it contains, the Firmament, the Heavens and the Earths, the worlds underground, all the paradises and hells, this means that the whole of the universe is to be found there in that Earth in its entirety, and yet the whole of it together is like a ring lost in one of our deserts in comparison with the immensity of that Earth. And that same Earth has hidden in it so may marvels and strange things that their number cannot be counted and our intelligence remains dazed by them. . . .

A multitude of things exist there which are rationally impossible, that is, a multitude of things about which reason has established decisive proof that they are incompatible with real being. And yet! – all these things do indeed exist in that Earth. It is the vast prairie where the theosopher-mystics feast their eyes; they move around in it, they go and come in as they will. In the whole of all the universes that make up that Earth, God has especially created one universe in our image (a universe corresponding to each of us). When the mystic contemplates the universe, it is himself, his own soul, that he contemplates in it. . . .

In that Earth there are gardens, paradises, animals, minerals – God alone can know how many. Now everything that is to be found on that Earth, absolutely everything, is alive and speaks, has a life analogous to that of every living being endowed with thought and speech.

The Book of the Spiritual Conquests of Mecca

BRING AVICENNA, LET HIM SING

Now let us do this. A long sailing, yes, as before; again,
                            a walking below the ground.
Avicenna crests and skims in shoes of olive shade, above soles of moon.
My father digs up and drags ten wheat fields through the full speaking
buck of Avicenna, loop de loop, as it somersaults and woozes,
a moaning and spiking machine whine of recital in powdered ground
                                    of stubble.
My father tumplines eight irrigation pipes
with Sumerian writing and threads them, snouts to tanks, he
headports southern Italy's dirt feet, a Safeway bag of ears.
The fields dragonfly over him white hair. Two men,
dancing like cranes, my father steroided by the grave.
And now we begin. A long sailing, as before,
                            a walking below the ground.
A wingspread sailing, his face sewn into my lip, our feathered mouth.
A bearded sailing.
Venus key-scratches a pentagram in five skies, everything inserts its head
     into the mouth of mathematics in the face of everything. All right,
we anneal that in, ballpeenly, one stroke, and Avicenna ladders up
in this song-bread now as it enters this oven.

I WILL SERVE

1

Understory and low rebar of crickets
   in wormhole grass on the face-gathering mountain.
Human spark bodies, ascetical with speed, look and look into the grass
                       chimneys and wolverine into them;
         they are salted with the dead skin of diesel exhaust.
Golden eagles flex chorally, snakes in their beaks,
                    just before the utterance
        of the continent waterfalls blackly over it and down.
The eagles thread into participation with the swaying, savoured ladder
of migration, the straits, their drive and slapping decay the first hold,
                        the first hold.
Hummingbirds grind in fuchsia forests.
The colonial move of the hand smokes like a garbage fire
at the top of the liver.

2

Even if we sent, in a movement of prayer, 5,000 contracted men, rolling
                   from trucks, off quads,
into the fir with vibrating knives, concordances, GPS, they could not
slide and labour to the mouth that moves on the wound, chip-dealing
swoon-bearing, nor would they be able to shell game it working up
the ice-opened valley where they would still smell
only the ice's old stacked miles of ice.

3

When the people scraped along the Siberian coast, I saw them,
in and out of hide boats (fur on the inside), west to east, bumping
                              along in black and white,
their lives footage of rotting film, they hung the tongue of corpses
between whale jaws, so if their dead began to sway and sound,
they would goat-roam in bending, rain-holding bones and these would
lead the words up, out of sliding till.

4

The winged objects, ivory, in the graves,
of running small stones, the faces
of those carved on the white flight spread, their
fishhead hands, were king-motioned to smooth the soul's shot
                                        through and in gravel,
to kiss upon it maximum weight, to breastfeed all wobble from it,
so choir-together movement-whisper along the Bering Flats.
Early winter glower spinally leaks from this ivory and shifts and sheets
                                        in sand, the eye
has the scent; it holds it above the shake of the earth.

Water off North Farm,
Vladivostok zebu-backed, seal grease-nippled, falling drumming,
wobbles over like a falling house, hands feet tied in the diesel
of its falling; bottomless beak, sleeping, travelling stone (*ousia*); this
is the live mousetrap of light, it is a bowl of charcoal flashes, faces of
animals as torches inside, they are looking inward then down from
                    moony galleries embedded within the sliding arc –
    the rose-fish salted with the salt of Plotinus comes –
Like a prison bus thighed with lightning, the electrically jellied monad
slapped over, one breath processing with cavalry jingle under flags in night's
                    plush theatre of joined thousands –
cougars with rhododendron stump eyes odiferous as jugged meat,
cats whose eyes carry the multiple swoons of planets, ether-breezes
of necessity; hecatombs of bulls in circles of church interiors and
mead halls, left buttock to right buttock weather, bodies will-magmaed
looking inward and down in transcendental deduction, the small-thick
minerals of the brows, the heroic night-magnetting turn;
they belt-slip around momentum's villageless circle and huzz toward us
opening and over and look in and what they are eats over our heads.
(The moons of animals fluxed in the upper water.)
A shortened wind of eyes devilling around an empty hub at the feathery
end of the lift, merganser crest of the sleepwalking, the flying,
falling, cakey street, one language, deep, all tendon – black insect belly,
    Odysseus' ship, moving quickly in it above us *oardip oardip oardip* –
breaking up in violent air and going into rain-burning trees alone ahead
                    of us.

A DRAGON FOR BENEDICT ON HIS FEAST

for W.L.

Bone topknotted, riveted, yellow clover
        crushed, oil-heavy bodies, Prayer
of the Heliotrope, prayer of the third century, wings dried egg
whites almost organs of vision, night church panes
               swaying in bomb suck.
Swollen dragonflies power calendars on their bodies.
Numerized, jumbotron bodies, diagnostic keys, gyroscopes
                  of happenstance's grain.
Inside this dragonfly, a crackling volcano goes up like an airshow,
muscle of insideness; down one slope, a 12x12 shack. Hello, sailor.
It slings in its body a shelf of bones.
The dragonfly humps in its immurement a shelf of other lucky bones.
Exact, not rational, it shakes
through its shell a closet of falling rocks and
                  a solar eclipse.

      *   *   *

Moon-dark of dying keeps staring at me; my mother goes back
into her too-windowed building, where meals are provided, shining
                  as one, howdahing
around the rotting family castle.
Here's a piece for me, here's a piece for Greg.
I'll take my part, let everyone know I'll pick it up, in reeds by the creek.

      *   *   *

The dragonfly rests on *The Rule of St. Benedict*
at noon in a blue, tight hall,
ausculata, ausculata, and as the thick-tongued blood kick
of dilation drops like wind at dusk,
the whiskery, bi-plane skeleton sinks, falling miles into the book.
Be the solder-mouth, swollen blue-gold fly, says the writing, here
still, just under these grass heads.

THEURGY II

I looked because Proclus and pseudo-Dionysius and Iamblichus
chained out their black geese tongues twirling; they shook over
night-lichened ground, double-axed, skirring in the insect-throated
music of the Gospel of St. John; they sent out their red-purple swan
tongues, moving, and I looked and armying out from burned seeing,
gold disjecta from glaciers, were standings and movings of
someone walked through by the river-stone barb of the seen things
and moving out were sweeps of arcing, a gold blood
decaying, faceless, stepping down, wing-folding, in the forehead,
for bucked in the heave of the tongue I looked at the statue of the
mountain and its thundery flowers and at the flowing statue

                                          of fish-shaken
dark behind the names of things, I looked and looked at the statue
of the idea palace, all those breathing candles, the almost unlit falling
into knowing's body, and at the statue of fast
speaking and at the statue of light quick layering in the mouth and at
the statue of walking.

My deaf, fox-faced cousin stared an afternoon of wind at me quivering
and slapped up in speech the tottering memory palace
           of Jack the Trapper digging into the side of a hill in the Thirties,
infant coyote jerking inside chicken wire fences in his silverweed yard
across the walkable lake from the thickening, novocained

                            hill where holy rollers
moaned and snaked under blankets, an oil
lamp flickering inside the hill, I looked at that and walked inside
the palace or city going up, heat lines, from that speaking, my mother
crying, wanting home, and away from the mewling soil, and I looked

and wore without knowing the apophatic tattoo which walked
                    out from that reversing, bravely reversing, light.

My deaf cousin rode into me the tattoo of the statue of crazy,
                              neighbourly Mary Kucherabi,
holding her dead mother in the house all winter, saying to callers
"Mom doesn't get around much any more," the skull in the bed rolling
from vertebrae with a rustle; stewing sauerkraut in the dead room,
offering it in handfuls to visitors, shaking it, *vinegar, be gone*, none
of whom saw the corpse-hump in covers, heating
the place with cheerful poplar till the end of May when moths broke
up from snow mould.

I looked and light dragged its Yoruba scars across the open mouth
and across seeing. Cities of speaking go up inside, *sursum agere*,
                              with violent horses, and
I move along beetling arms' width alleys, reading the scripture of blue
light inside my clothes, and begin to see a few feet upward,
                    the weight of the seen tipping down
on to stuttering pillars of shadow in seeing's bearded, stream-fast
                    engineering.

THE BOY, HE, CHURNING HIMSELF TO DIVINITY

> Having aroused himself for the reception of these men's [Zeno and
> Parmenides'] insight, having by his words unfolded and exhibited
> his fitness for partaking of it, he [the young Socrates] stops speaking
> and begins to receive the midwifely instruction that they give him.
> — Proclus, *Commentary on Plato's Parmenides*, II.V.781

The seven languages glistening on vellum,
unspeaking, looking spearthrows ahead, what combed backs
                              they have, what thunder-hording backs, the
ant-flicker of DNA in the languages trickle-knotting into a dream of a
                              single neck-bleeding
animal or an animal bleeding from the mouth, chanting from a book,
the coyote-pitched sound, eaten in wind then suddenly back,
the blood-balled white goat throat.
Chaldean, chainsawed and hammered Aramaic with winks
    of Castillean apprentice skin stunned inside (Moses de Leon, I see you!),
the languages are cities almost touching on a plain, summer-polished
night, Calgary and its outriders, say, the languages,
building in growing dilation flight-pathing from the east, the inching,
flexed-with-necessity long reindeer bodies of the careless languages.
Now it is possible to hear the furred gears of a great eye
as it rumbles above the night sward of the book,
humid plain, bronze-working fires below,
the great eye at balloon height circling with a mild machine
                              throat clearing,
then, ahead, an aural mountain range which is the cosmos rehearsed
in Proclus' NASA countdown voice, the ladders of names travelled up
                    and down.

A road of riprap rises into Cappadocian high country, a motorcycle,
the reader riding pillion.
From dunes lifts a casino tower, *The Philosophy of Science* scrolling
                in red pixels across the top.
Thinking is here in silos of wind,
wind shrugged from the moon.
Here thinking is pushed out, waving ropes of thinlipped marrow
                from the languages.

FR. PAUL LE JEUNE, S.J., IN THE FOREST

Quebec Relation, 1633

They skim on birchbark
roofs, porting two weeks of shunting moons,
or head-basketing all forests' nights and the bailed hair of winds.
They are spoken to by their demonic friend,
the other moon of four yard ice ramming its horn
along the river's groove.
One of them saw gouged in the 14 foot wall
he'd just climbed in sleep, mucusy, flowing, the law
he must eat me with an edge he'd flaked from the obsidian
of 3:00 a.m., and so behead the reptile rumbling under his skin.
He sank his axe under fish scales in his yellow bed two weeks.
His wife flew me away with her eyes.
He counted the wasps behind his lids; in the tinder
of deerflies in his room he rubbed
his two droughted fingers.
Five gouts of enemy pneumatic flame
scuffed above him, slamming as a pen of steers,
he in limey bed furs.

a   *o*   *e*   I work for the world to rise
into the breathholes of my speech.
When I walked back to our community along the water,
the statue of Kateri Tekakwitha, burnt an inch in,
swayed from the longhouse fire,
missiled hissing from the river through thinnest ice,
runnelling mud and spawn.

We tar the boats for their children
whom they hide to be worked to France.
Their divinations' yellow wings
fan through the roar of leaves.

Suhrawardī

When you learn from the writings of the ancient Sages that there exists a world possessed of dimensions and extent, other than the pleroma of Intelligences and the world governed the by Souls of the Spheres, and that in there are cities beyond number among which ... [are] Jabālqā and Jabārsā, do not hasten to proclaim it a lie, for there are pilgrims of the spirit who come to see it with their own eyes and in it find their heart's desire. As for the rabble of imposters and false priests, they will deny what you have seen even if you bring proof to expose their lie. Therefore, remain silent and have patience....

Book of Conversations

Suhrawardī

A narrative and a dream: For some time I was prey to an intense obsession. I ceaselessly practiced meditation and spiritual exercises, since the problem of knowledge assailed me with insoluble difficulties. What they say about it in books brought me no light. On one particular night I experienced a dreamlike ecstasy. Suddenly I was wrapped in gentleness; there was a blinding flash, then a very diaphanous light in the likeness of a human being. I watched attentively and there he was: Helper of souls, Imam of wisdom, *Primus Magister*, whose form filled me with wonder and whose shining beauty dazzled me. He came toward me, greeting me so kindly that my bewilderment faded and my alarm gave way to a feeling of familiarity. And then I began to complain to him of the trouble I had with this problem of knowledge.

"Come back (awaken) to yourself," he said to me, "and your problem will be solved."

"How so?" I asked.

"Is the knowledge which you have of yourself a direct perception of yourself by yourself, or do you get it from something else...?"

Book of Elucidations

The quick black flag of your name jumps to your eyes.
You are in the cave of infection, pewter
    sleep in a drift of flint points pounded under surf
        gravel at the back of a rock fold.
It is starting to speak.
A burning man rocks at the mouth in the new moon's curved shoe;
        leave the Manichean alone.
The Baltic is melting.
You are in the heron-scarred fish of infection under water flab.
You are in the rolling antler of infection
    hucked over fire, spurted by a man's feet.
The stunned forests cry south.
You are nailed on infection's column,
homesteading from flame on its one ocular tooth.
People feed you by rope.
The doors have seen the bird of your name though it is disguised
        as reindeer moss.
You wear infection's gown which is MacKenzie Delta light, it's yours,
skin, an ice-scarred name. It goes in and out
    of you, tree to tree, to eyebranch.
Which is caribou light.
You are on infection's horse, on its instant shadow, your name
        flies
into and out of the animal's sawing mouth.

Snow-smoke, black-towel-wrapped river-knives shaken,
    and wolf-scraped snow, gnarled with night's burnt-house urine,
                          cleft-smoke,
bound-foot-valley smoke, dead bee hills and hills of dead bulls,
yellow tallow hill breath and the straw-smelling black stone.
In the inner skin, under the filing river, under the eyelid, in the
dimpled hum, skin swarm, in the base place, ear-combed, shouldery
with shadow, a bowed tattoo of motion,
the eyelid tattoo which is a club of star-smoke.
Now you find the eye's shoulder-wide, furred hole: now
                     lower your hips into the rising-to-applaud place,
now the cow-eyed, dolphin-eyed hips are the hero corm.
And you walk down stones of icon's eyes,
               infection's crow riding the cloud seam as speech, and you
skid on your ass down the mudded incline to the pulse of cosmology
                   wobbling off the wall, poulticed by burning fish,
and now, just as you are leaving, under stone, you see it, under a leaf
                  on the needled floor, a stare left behind by
                      an Orthodox slave.
The night pulls out each feather of the eye. The eye's wingbones
are buried in night's mouth,
dug out later, shaken on the ground, read,
then flicked into the trees by long sticks.

A room, then a room, of Soviet machinery shelved in the two
                                    big antibiotic tablets.
The worm door, waterskinned, dimples and craters.
Glass falls through glass outside the brick.
Cheerful, literal lugnuts fat with history's caloric force, goitred
    foodprocessors with exoskeleton cutting bars, the face, the face,
    turning away, of Reason.
Down the hatch, down, *kataban*, you go to jerking fires
                                    and the sex-breathed kelp beds.
Out of the pills, unpacked by the simply hungry, teleology's black
                    ribbon jutters forward in oyster-midden cloud.
Shave or they won't give you morphine.
The road gathers greenness, you are loyal to the bed, coldwelded
                    forehead blur, loyal to the sheet.
The nose-holes of the 1:00 a.m. charred animal who fisted before you
                under the mountains, cigar rolls of winds,
are the meaty, tail-whipping tunnels.   *Get ready.*   *Now.*

BRUISE

Single-celled light, grass a long walk in snow from wheat,
the end of it, shouts in its sleep,
lifting its drawbridge, and over your skin, becoming
your skin, mossed rock machine-hums into place; a bee-eye vial
of tight no-longer-seeing is slivered into you through
the morphine portal in your left thigh
and you are coaxed to follow it in.
If there are chairs ahead, they will be made of arrows.
Now immediately you inch under medieval grass
and in the bruxist grass the robe-whisper
of people who cannot read. Their porridgy, flowing,
plasmic dreams must become your food, politics, school.
If you open your wallet now, the cards
inside will be faces that hold noses and mouths
from beyond the haired doors.

Sunflowers, wet sparrows,
grind in their throats into a vinegar fog over the ground,
where Pythagoras lies, stroking the bear,
putting fruit and bread into its mouth, whispering to it;
they're on the second terrace, under the dried Chinese lantern plants,
disguised a dog-range invisibilities, fox not quite turned
                              into people, the last Final Causes;
in the bear's skull, the ordered light returns
and rims correctly. Pythagoras has planted
three two by fours into the bear, who has been eating people recently,
                    to fingernail the cosmos' veering, fluid weight,
until Being's own speed treasurechest will cradle it.
Fruit and bread, touching the hair around the mouth.
The bear scents the swooping slosh of crowned, deeply thighed light
that corners and corners in him; he will soon follow a braid of it
                    up the gathering mountain,
and we, in the houses, will taste our sickness rising
              on ladders from our skin lakes.

Nine a.m. moon over the Frank Slide,
sturgeon-spined rocks freezing the valley,
the right of the moon a third broken off,
Iamblichus on its shoulder, an arrows-of-light-passed-through
bird, muttering.
Sandbar flicker. In the ear of this
is the knowing of the stub-winged shadow
foreheading from the east side of the mid-Pacific,
thudding a yard below the water, it
shivers toward the Goat River, clicking
into the Sweetgrass Hills, its hands red, the soles of its feet red,
then rumbles back below the ground.
We want to call this into our faces on needles of the contrails of wasps.
The hills are low eyes in a pillish,
masking mist.
Buffalo scent in the sleep of the shoulders of the new webs
in the yard, such sleep in the underwater lime of the new cliff ferns.
The darkness wound my feet, hands
    torso, hips in salt-floured felt, sealed with
beeswax and shop-lifted me into its thorax.
The Motion in a crown of hail, in a
    crown of arthritic blackberries,
the moving, quarter-mouthed, eighth-mouthed, gill-growing back.

At the water line, at the eye mark
across the calabash containing the trash of the seen, then a falling
   of three steps to where a backflipping, arms-spread slop of old blood
     curls down like a god's brown greased beard,
iris-scan the hole –
    forty below jellying of caribou gouged
         with breath-lines;
    a falling, combed hand, alone, slanting across
      the rain screen of the eye-shoving valley;
    swans lifting, powdering water,
      Lake Athabasca, April new snow on the banks;
    the clip-rattle of an AK-47 bunked in ice.
The loose hand floats to your face,
a song's heat wave is secreted to dark objects, John Stuart Mill
power-take-offs into his sideburn whorls, Gerard Manley Hopkins
Titans from a chair, scissors to you, a stacked milk glass
   of a dream of kicking you in the balls fingertipped before him.
Silver cones tongue up in low thunder, then
        the Siberian coast,
weather-drum, salmon-beaked,
Neanderthal forehead of weather. Yes,
to i.v. train wreck via your nuts would marry
delight to terror press, press the bees against the forehead wall
of Edmund Burke, then to drive the car over your hand.

The Child buried on the swan's wing,
and the pelagic divinity coughing in its beard of bells

are inside the rock-sliding-on-rock weather of the other place,
the dusking voice, swan-plumbed, of that world's weather,
        its mouth, mound of turquoise duff, begins.

COMBAT

They mine sheets of light and smelt what they find on the beach
by the ships, and others are on the seaward infected hump
                                        of the trench,
the ground runs fever, and they comb hair out of the wind
to make their fabulous rugs, calling the fever into them.
Hello, Don, I can see you looking for me at the Ross Bay bar, but
I'm ditzing in the eighth climate, I know you can see it, too,
above the silver rash of the senses and above the glassy flame scar
under the rash of the delectations of the ingenious holes and under
the plutonium hand signs, bows, door
openings in the lodge of Lord Intelligence, which are compass marks
    and prompts cut on the jewelled air's body there,
where they mine light with fishbone, fake eyelash steel
                                        on drumskin sand,
and comb from wind their leaping rugs in medio mundus.
And against this, the grasses' drunkenness
and against this the grasses' inebriated war
and that river, the Cowichan, falling into the body of the angel of its
turn round a basalt lump, dragging a knotted shirt of moths.
And still against this, against this, the hero's cougarish sulk, *that* world,
                                        crimson imaginalis,
flyingsaucers from the brow, in a hearable robe, shoulder balls of
                                        rufous towhees.
It pelicans from caught breath, citying.
It swells in supine eyesacks well-clavicled music.

COULEE, EAGLE CREEK

Turtle, damp with rising, lemony with the sweat which is
    the light of being seen, bruised and slurred with weight, pierced,
    thick-tongued as an airliner wadding from the burnt underland;
turtle pictographed with a score of a drum solo of falling from the sky,
    that has had breathed into its nostrils the scar of falling down,
jerks itself from the grass, its arthritis oceanic, hello, hello, leaking
uncaking shadows, cooling from its life in the other place.
Hello, hello, an ear at last given,
a room at last in a stone house,
a spine inside, waiting, of an unswept afternoon,
hollyhock spine, breath-pillar from five feet in the ground.
Turtle limestoned from pressed smoke in herd-cut grass.
Up in the hills where buffalo squeezed
like toothpaste from the earth, jellied up,
the bees of their testes moving, the on-the-money
                          homeruns of their horns, moving,
the argument against realism, its mildly drugged loll,
                          files its teeth.
A cloud cuts a notch in the earth's neck,
there is so much to fear.
In the field below the worked out coal seam, one stallion,
                    five mares and a colt, until, near evening
Europeans and their bibles come softening into animal grass.
The eye of the creek holds everything where it is, and strokes
each self-forgotten, illuminist child of light until it
                          untremors in its skin-down,
moths whose backs are landslides,
the dusk moon falling through its spyhole.

Hello, hello, a room where you dress in flicker feathers
and brownthrasher feathers and lie down, mouth and half your throat
full of the quills of your grandfather's and grandmother's
and your infant aunt's bones.

HE HOLDS

Randy hammers on *Humanae Vitae*, you've
just got to give everything.
The furred, garbage-stink mass bulled the saw in the surgeon's hand
when it moved its shoulders, scent-howling, and swayed west
                                    from behind his ears.
Then it pitched his tent in 150 degree light.
Seven foot non-sequentiality is a machine, fished from the grass,
of transformation, cleavering the hand darting
to discursivity. He holds his own hand
in seizure. I'll take this dance.
Let me tell you about the Oil Sands. Wrong, wrong.
What the hell's the matter with nuclear, a reac-
tor in all the four corners. They have this new
doohickey, piece of pie, *techne*, new planet that eats yellow cake
to a few crumbs in the forest.
If he'd sleep his arm in Asclepius' moon burrows
If he'd send the mother bear from the top of him to speak with
         glow in the forest clearing
If he'd loan the lunge of his arm, not effing likely, to night
out, deal its cards, under the tiles of the hissing lair
The Baltimore Catechism – absolutely quick-shuffle true
but what does it tell us about the way truth vines round and through
                              the tongue?
Move quickly, move quickly in this soft-quick
triumphal car round the wind-made pool table.
He lands, many, on certainty's spike.
Levis currus, the sublime skin, double clutches,
revs its mill and begins the fishtail turn.

69

Satan fears me, though he has a forest
        in his mouth. I know the key.
If the abbot broke out guns, the Hells Angels
wear a target on their backs, we'd go hunting bikers.
He holds his own hand in seizure, blood, the mouth, *dictata rosa*,
inside his mouth.
We're talking the Epiphany of the Imam,
        more or less, amigo, or Parousia in backflip.
What do you say? Hero or zero? You snooze, you lose.

If he'd evacuate his arm's occult
gymkhana, its spy-ish falconry to the one safe place among the trees.

COGNITIO MATUTINA

Bugaboo Mountains

Army of glow, shouts
of massed wasps, axle whicker, original
wave – pine pollen, scarves of krill – elected light,
semened in stones.

And the prairie breathes before the eastern range,
dragonflies and sloughs, alkali pans, blue clays,
pictographs, welding flashes, avocet and brine shrimp, pesticide
                    prongs stepping above and away
          from the curve of the sprayers' skirts.
And here, in the horn-light of leaves,
the glaciers are in growling katabasis.
Bald and bearded, the glaciers shaking and walking backwards
          down the cellar stairs.

And in the light, boats of anemone, and in the
boats, women the size of small fingers
launch forward, slacken up in sweeps.
From the palms of these, hummingbirds.
From the palms, falcons, appearing now, curving rock,
from the palms, young larches.
Women in the flowers' hairy boats.
The nation floats in stone-scented light.
And behind this light, light's disciplined skin,
     then occluded, jammed light, then light
rusticated to homesteads in stone,

laid under the tongue there, then behind
and below this light, nothing and under the
nothing, nothing, then nothing with a minor perfume, as
clouds auto-wreck and nose-roll their bodies
up the spike called Snow-patch.

A plain of ice-dressed granite,
curved shoulder, lichen headdressed stone, albumined,
now and then, haloed with goats' breath.
Lichen headdressed, the glacier's clickety-click bones.
Locked moraine fontain,
the glacier, puckering waspnest slowing into low talk with itself,
the glacier, ice beard, with itself.
Force, aristocratic, rock-river
that takes the fork of the human body.

Bearded glacier, where there is horn-light on leaves
and larks have two-thirds climbed the ghost wall at 8,000 ft.,
woolly everlasting yellow-tipping, coltsfoot yellow-tipping,
and the pine-tar moon come to moan its smoke
over the demons of Cobalt Lake.

[*OEDIPUS has entered*]

FIRST EPISODE

OEDIPUS: You pray! Then listen:
What you pray for you can have –
    remission of these miseries and help
    if you'll hear my plan:
    a plan to stop the plague.
I speak of course as a stranger to the story
    and a stranger to the crime,
    being too late your latest citizen
And helpless, therefore to track it very far
    unless you lend me clues.
Wherefore, I boldly challenge
    all you Thebans here with this:
Does any man among you know
    who killed Laius son of Labdacus?
Such a one I now command
    to tell me everything.

[*He waits for a reply*]

If self-incrimination keeps him silent
    let him be assured
He need fear nothing worse than banishment
    and he can depart unharmed.

[*He pauses again*]

Perhaps one of you is aware
    the murderer was someone from some other land.
Let him not be shy to say it.
I shall heap rewards on him,
    besides my deepest blessing.

[*No one stirs*]

What, silent still?

Sophocles, *Oedipus the King*

Socrates

But you we have begotten for yourselves and for the rest of
the city like leaders and kings in hives; you have been better
and more perfectly educated and are more able to participate
in both lives. So you must go down, each in his turn, into the
common dwelling of the others and get habituated along with
them to seeing the dark things.

Republic, 520b–c

Marble billowing, opera's sweet curve at dusk, *The Critique of Judgment*,
          its perfect posture pacing in a lit window, genius' highvoiced
headdress, Canada Bereft, all the storefront rash,
and below site rubble, weightlessness' bruise ridging into a bloom,
                    which hisses like a severed main.
A man walks into endless pasture, the Industrial Revolution a throaty
thistle-wind that looses arrow-falls of language in himself to himself
                    – it clutches the jaw, breathing
into the drowned man mouth – and, pneuma-wheel, cranks the legs.
All the metal blowing through the air, flicking palm oil like a shaking dog,
all the metal blowing through air, but its prince is eye-drop feedable
                    like a pre-weaner raccoon.
Leave him. The empty quarter in objects jet-ejects through shells
or just drive-the-car-into-the-wall wishes itself away.
Infection pounds over him like one of three caribou herds.
But a snake mouth of gas, sworded.
Dig him a hole.
The big engine redlines a mouth-rush
at *Zarathustra*, swallowing it into an Ikea manual, and pulls the chord,
                    mounting the show.
So tonic into him, bad cholesterol, yes, but still, a wall-eye read
                    Book of Revelation,
he'll soften and spread his legs as he sniffs the glue of the mathematics.
Arc in further stones and fill, asphalt floes, how
          he moves, fan
of gravel dealing out the ass of the chunking forward double axle,
how he moves.
The bridal knife waits in her room, thinking: his atomicity,
          that building body.

POLITICS, ANAGOGIA

— a libretto —

Dramatis Personae
Iamblichus: 4th century Syrian neo-Platonist, author of *On the Mysteries*
Proclus: 5th century diadochus, author of *The Platonic Theology*
Carl Brewer: defenceman, Toronto Maple Leafs, 1960s

Iamblichus: He wakes soon to the writhe of bulls, bulls, bulls
on his mouth's flocked roof.
When the ricochet forehead singularity wakes, it will be as froth
in their brown-black wind.
Proclus: He wakes. And kicks away from the drug's leaking wall.
There he is, knuckly man, his lateral blur face scratching through
stones' pelt.
And, again, there he is. A smoky bell
on caribous' antlers, mountaining and valleying.
Iamblichus: He will come up.
We will speak him through the crusts.
The magnet of our talk will whorl him until
his face is horns. We will suck the ground for him.
Carl Brewer (under the earth, slurred, wavering): And the talk which
was everywhere
in sawblade fern in deer mice,
Proclus: — squided, minked through with Dionysius' legs and arms —
Carl Brewer: It went on coming from walls,
factoryish dark, where I wormed into a pounded fire, nuded itself

on cups of water, on cups of motor oil, and
on motion-salvering walls,
stilted through the smudge four nights,
careening and pry-barring at every ledge.
The bowing speech deceived me from the clubbing
of a leaf, leaf's shadow on my face, from a life under
the facial bruise of a concussive
world and its laws.
   308 tons of earth and engine parts above me were a flick of a hand.
Iamblichus: The boy wakes with a spider in his mouth,
the lurch of bulls, bulls burnt across the roof of his mouth.
Carl Brewer: Then a man came, unbelievably quick, slouched, moving
at a third his height, baggy with vowels, stunning
from mineral, a pulsing mile deep spin and jump and step back,
and he flensed (how?)
the ropes from our necks.
Iamblichus: This man's mouth moved with pounding sideway speed,
haycutter blade mouth.
He looked like he would take the boy's neck into the blaze and
chipping sparks but he landmined away the rope,
and he put two fingers in the septum
of the boy and he dragged him to his feet.
Carl Brewer: Then we were lifted in a hall of bad wings,
moths, sliced plastic lampshades, jimmied against
our metal dust skins, there were many and we
were in freightliners of shitting steers, shit-soaked
ice around the dysentery wash of steers
on kicking highways, south, snow.
Proclus: And speech was against them like a
clutch plate, calming and honeymooning into them and then
they brightened with speed to another air.

Carl Brewer: We walked days on what seemed a glacier, there was
   a rocky throat slimed with moss from which gouged,
   cloth-ripped pneumatic shouts, I rise
   in aging smoke,
   smoke's spider on my calf
   and then, o that, that, the sun wave-lifted into us with its hammer
                                        five times, the
   five times, five times
   and the gruffing steer sides and jaws flipped from us swerving, each
   with their winds. Eye's jelly hummocked with what stain-leapt
   forward thus worldingly in.
   We later spoke to the tribes nearby through the tunnel
                                    of their red paint
   and they took a ladlelike needle and worked us back
   into the ground.

Dead fuchsia and carrots still not growing through winter
in the wood-chipped garden hump, each swivels up its own radio
                              station and heaves
out honey; in everything hair-on-the-back-of-the-neck
lit ash spiralling out maquettes of the whole milkish machine; in
everything a carved book to which abalone has been sewn,
with a postal address and a SIN number, on a lectern of antler
at which a throat-cut lamb singingly reads aloud;
in everything limestone arguing; in everything, in everything; in
everything suddenly a river that cannot be crossed, the lowest eye
                              looks at you
until you feel a walnut of gravity frowning down in your elbow;
Hermes with a sharp stick
scratching the ground in everything, in everything the Gulf of Alaska
        in its wire.
In Fawn Lily's underarm bloom, a swimming sound.
Indian Plum now holds the vase of seeing, which poured out is Hermes.
In everything this answering machine tripping again its loop, please
                              leave me
a message; in everything a billet doux under a book; in everything the
lost sock; and a sound comes up from the spoon under the bed,
pieces of dental floss, idiorhythmic chorale,
totus Christus, and out of this creeps a city with four nameless rivers.
In everything ignorance, *docta ignorantia*, last bus stop
on the line of Dionysian apophaticism, the black door opens
hydraulic exhalations, home at last, do not look back.
In everything, listen, the Shriners' parade, Regina, 1961, just ended;

rain starts to hit into the dust, then the fog of the god; in everything, the self-wealthing rooms, and in them the sidelong, fish-profile boxes on coffee tables, mouthing out meals and fire without a mind.

ACKNOWLEDGMENTS

Some of these poems were published earlier in *Prism International*, *The Malahat Review*, *Arc*, *The Walrus*, and *The Literary Review of Canada*. "Cognitio Matutina" was written for the film *In the Stone Scented Light*, conceived by Davida Monk and filmmaker Arthur Nishimura, choreographed by Davida Monk, with dancers Amelia Itcush and Alanna Lemieux, and Allan Gordon Bell as composer.

My deep thanks go to Don McKay – for the editing and for the conversation.

*

The extracts from Plato's *Phaedrus* on pages 11-12 and 21-23 are from the translation by Alexander Nehamas and Paul Woodruff. Copyright © 1995 by Alexander Nehamas & Paul Woodruff. Reprinted by permission of Hackett Publishing Company, Inc. All rights reserved.

The extracts from Iamblichus' *De mysteriis* on page 29-30 are from the translation by Emma C. Clarke, John M. Dillon, and Jackson P. Hershbell. Copyright © 2003 by the Society of Biblical Literature. Reprinted by permission of the Society of Biblical Literature.